TIDINGS

Tidings

A Christmas Journey

RUTH PADEL

Chatto & Windus
LONDON

1 3 5 7 9 10 8 6 4 2

Chatto & Windus, an imprint of Vintage,
20 Vauxhall Bridge Road,
London SW1V 2SA

Chatto & Windus is part of the Penguin Random House group of companies whose
addresses can be found at global.penguinrandomhouse.com

First published by Chatto and Windus in 2016

www.vintage-books.co.uk

A CIP catalogue record for this book is available from the British Library

ISBN 9781784741068
Printed and bound by C&C Offset Printing Co., Ltd., China

Penguin Random House is committed to a sustainable future for our business, our
readers and our planet. This book is made from Forest Stewardship Council®
certified paper.

For Dr Sushrut Jadhav, the team
at Focus Homeless Outreach and Street Population, Camden,
and their work with those who are marginalised
and have no voice

CONTENTS

Voices

CHAROUM	The Angel of Silence
HOLLY	A seven-year-old girl
ROBIN	A homeless man of forty-four
FOX	A young female fox
MESOMA	A volunteer in a Christmas homeless centre

CHRISTMAS EVE

The Voice of Silence

T am the oldest angel, the dark side of the brain.
Everything untold, suppressed, unseemly or wild
is under my protection. I am Charoum,
Angel of Silence. I am the seed of fire
in a hearth you thought was cold,
the stillness when you step into moonlit snow
and who you are in private. I appear
whenever you drop into quiet, when surface
cracks, lustre and veneer rub thin.
Silence, you say, when you make room for wonder.
I am less and less here. But tonight, for twenty-four
strange hours in the darkness of the year, I have a voice –

for this is Christmas Eve, when everything hidden
comes alive. Children's toys
that have rolled under a sofa, or stayed
in the cupboard unplayed-with for years,
the mice you weren't aware of in the wall,
and your own unspoken longing to be given
something more by life: suddenly, if you listen,
all unnoticed things can talk. And so can I. Tonight
I play a part in everyone's secret search

for something better. Come with me
to St Pancras Old Church, on a little London hill
runed with twenty centuries of human stories.

Nearby shops are closing on Camden High Street,
Euston Road. The sky is that bruise-colour
you hardly think *is* sky, and sodium lights
from the station terminal
flicker in glass sides of the bus shelter
like a zodiac on mica.
London's neon glory falls
on wet-purple tarmac of Royal
College Street and its last-minute traffic:
on roadworks, traffic cones, surveillance
cameras above the door of a homeless hostel
and the final Eurostar before the Christmas break.

Below us, evening pads down Pancras Road
and pokes its nose through shy, half-open doors
of girls tying last-minute mistletoe
in Goldington Crescent, Unity Mews, Penryn
while young men fresh from the gym
zip back the first ring-pull of lager.

Up here the evening glides over golden moss
on the flat-top tomb of Mary Wollstonecraft
where her daughter – whom she never knew,
and died giving birth to – met her lover, Shelley,
in secret. And here is the Hardy Tree
where a young surveyor, not yet a writer,
ordered to clear consecrated land
to make the new thing, Railway, fanned
dug-up grave-stones like slices of grey bread
round a sapling ash in a memorial wheel.
Now the roots, look, flow and tentacle
through crumbled names on lichened marble.

People are trickling through the gates, up the path,
around the monuments and into church: a stream
of fur-trimmed anoraks and trailing scarves
for the Children's Service. Those two figures,
hurrying because they're late,
are Sue and her daughter, Holly.
Holly is seven. She's a pony,
prancing on the fire-fly shimmer
of LED *Light-Bringer* trainers
through a thousand-year-old arch
into an ancient shrine, built over a Roman altar
on the bank of the River Fleet –

long covered-over like the secret hopes, hidden
in every soul, which might flare out tonight
in joy or disappointment, in a loneliness
hardest to accept this time of year,
or else might bear new fruit.
That's why I'm here. I belong with secrets
kindly kept. With possibilities, with mute –

    for what might a mysterious birth, witnessed
by distant shepherds and foreign kings,
the longings conjured up by *giving*, *gift* and *given*
and this time-stopping rift in every schedule –
yes, what can Christmas do, to all of us?

Out of the Bushes

*C*hildren's voices singing *The First Nowell*
    ring out from the little church. Dark air whirrs
like the string of a plucked guitar. Think everyone
loves singing carols? Think again. This hill,
this park, seem empty now
but I'm watching for a man
who never makes a sound. Keep an eye
through sudden drizzle, on laurels
at the far edge of the graveyard
shadowed by St Pancras Hospital.
Those glazed, hard, lonely leaves of evergreen
are where mad homeless Robin likes to hide.

He's quarrelled with the world. I saw him gaze
at children going into church as if they
were shadow-puppets, nothing to do with him.
Now they've gone he shuffles from his cave.

Forty-four. His hair
is floating grease-locks, black and grey.
His face is beaten copper, smocked with red.
Wander-startled, as if he had a bounty

on his head. His stare
reminds you of a loose wind vane
flapping on a yacht in open sea.
There's a lot he can't, or won't, remember.
One careless glance at him can drown
his soul in thunder. He spends his days
round here, or down in town, but he goes to ground
in the muddled night of Sue and Bill's front garden.

They don't know he stashes a sleeping-bag
and rucksack, everything he owns,
under their shed, behind a tangle
of weed-cuttings and bramble –

and, like Saint Jerome, beds down there
with an animal – a young vixen he's tamed.
Or maybe she tamed him. She's company,
she keeps him safe. She's here too –
see her by that grave
hoping for food? But Robin
is catching echoes of his childhood.
Poor shepherds in fields they lay.
Robin has slept in those cold fields. He knows
the tunes. But remembering is danger.

Any way back in or any whiff of home,
is lost in muddy vales of wandering.

Babe in the manger, outcast and stranger.
The drizzle has turned to sleet, coming hard
like a spill of coins. Every breeze,
even the dab of air on his face as he shifts his feet,

will make him colder. There's hazard
everywhere. That's why he takes pains
to hide. Even the weather
is out to get him. *O Come All Ye Faithful?*
No. Shut out from all of that.
He lives on the cold side of alone
and never talks. Now, in the sleet,
he's watching pearls
                    of nearly-not-melting
                                        ice
roll off eaves of the Coroners Court.
Step closer. Listen to his thoughts.

>   *Church door's open. Could go in.*
>   *Been in once. Wood rafters like a stable.*
>   *Sick-sweet incense smell, a stone*

floor like a street, a staring boy
with a leopard at his feet
and a skull on the wall
with wings. Nothing like chapel at home.

Home. Where did that word come from?
Journey of a wound. At fourteen
Robin *cut and ran* – that's what he tells
himself – from an alcoholic mum,
a blank where his father might have been,
a Bible-bashing step-dad
and the darkness in between.

Can't we reach out and touch him? May this church
on its dark hill, spark-strung with golden windows
and humming with Europe's sweetest, oldest songs,
pass through his lonely fears to buried dreams
and kindle some unburnt thing in him that longs
to change. Behind this freezing layer of cloud
a billion stars spin over all our heads, unseen.

A Wolf in the Carol Service

*T*he church smells sweet, of forest and cut pine.
    Holly's sitting by a cardboard angel
with green eyes and silver wings, dangling a scroll

embroidered with gold words –
Goodwill to Men on Earth –
over Mary, Joseph, Baby Jesus,

seven shepherds, sheep and three Wise Men
whose turbans, wine-red cloaks and painted skin
say how foreign they are, how far away they're from.

Away in a manger. Why *away*? She can't wait till
    tomorrow.
She wrote her Father Christmas letter weeks ago.
What she's wishing for is her own

live, bright-eyed puppy. Bible words
float over her like pollen. *Governor of Syria.*
Mum's worrying whether Nan will get here safe alone.

That all the world be taxed. Is the tree up, at home?
The tub keeps falling over. *No room at the inn.*
The fairy lights won't light: Dad stayed to fix the fuse.

And this shall be a sign. Holly's brother Sam refused
to come. *Silent Night.* Pause. *Holy Night.* Sam said
carols were boring. *God on high.* Pause. *Draweth nigh.*

But this is magic night. *A lowly cattle shed.*
The night things come alive
and who knows what's round the corner?

> *Dear friends*, intones the priest,
> His voice is soft, like fur.
>
> *Blessed Saint Francis said*
> *every church is Bethlehem*
>
> *every altar is a manger.*
> *Once upon a time, this night*
>
> *was called Watch Night*
> *because the Angels came*

to tell the good news Christ was born
while shepherds watched their sheep

to protect them from danger
like lions, leopards and wolves.

Holly sees a wolf, pink tongue bendy as dough,
spreading panic through the *papier maché* sheep.
Outside, Robin shelters in the porch and listens too.

The Holy Family were travellers
turned away and sleeping rough.

Our patron, Saint Pancras,
was an immigrant to Rome.

He was a child, like you. A boy, fourteen,
from Phrygia – next door to Syria.

Let us pray tonight for travellers
and everyone who's lost their home.

Holly prays for that. Then extra, for a puppy.
In the deep midwinter, frosty wind made moan.
Her wolf is creeping up the aisle. He's shy,

he wags his tail - low, as dogs do
when they're uncertain. Look,
he likes her. Suddenly he's gone.

A reading from Saint Matthew.
The star stood over where He lay.

Wise Men, warned in a dream
departed another way.

Dear friends, we must remember
the wood of the manger will one day

give place to the wood of the Cross.
Glory be to God.

Holly wriggles. Christmas Eve is holding breath.
Christmas Eve is wrapping paper, secrets
and treasures she and Sam see once a year

and then forget. Has Nan come yet?
Have the fairy lights come on? And will she
get the lucky silver in the pudding, or will Sam?

What's True? How Do You Know?

*P*eople are pouring out of church, friends
    from Holly's class, neighbours she doesn't know
but they kiss her anyway, and everyone is smiling.
Have you hung up your stocking yet? Goodnight.
Goodnight. Now Holly's walking back with mum.
In Goldington Crescent Park
she spots an animal, not a dog or cat
but wild, she can tell,
like a wolf but smaller, beside a man
slumped over the fake boulder
Holly likes to climb. He is just sitting there, like stone,
in the dark, in the freezing rain. But now she's home

and the house is suddenly mysterious,
smelling of cinnamon
               pine-cones
                   secrets
                       Nan's *eau de cologne.*
Dad's got the new fire to work, real flames
with pretend logs. Will Father Christmas
like it? Sam is sure he'll come. The tree
touches the ceiling. In the firelight,

branches dance with shadow. No one minds
pine-needles on the carpet, not tonight,
and everything is gold and red and green.

Stand with me, watch Holly touch
with one finger-tip the shimmering balls
she remembers from last year when she was six.
When the door opens they rustle, click and shift.
On top is a silver star. Under a spangled fall
of rainbow lights are tinsel glitter-twists
and Cupids (I can't call them angels) playing gold-
frosted violins and harps. Here are four
crystal birds with tail-feathers like noodles
mum says are glass, spun-glass, and a white reindeer
in a sleigh. Holly has forgotten the man she saw
in the dark, on the sculpture-boulder, in the cold.

Come upstairs with Holly to the two
stockings Nan has knitted from sparkly wool.
Karen, at school, says her Da sneaks into her room
when she's asleep to fill her stockings. Is that true?
How do you know? For three days – that's special too –
Holly will be sleeping on Sam's floor, so Nan
can have her bed. Holly has arranged

three *My Little Ponies* on a chair. She can't go
to sleep without Twilight Sparkle, Rainbow Glow
and Star-Hopper, her favourite, turquoise with tinsel yellow
mane and tail. Christmas is really here! Tomorrow
she'll have a puppy, and these stockings will be full.

Tightrope

*R*obin is wandering towards the Thames,
  tunnelling in bins for food. The bus stop –
call that a seat? It's a slash of lipstick
in the dark. Too curved to lie on and too thin.
You can't rest there a minute, you'd slip off.
Christmas is the salt mine.
Salt in the wound, a nothing-time.
I was loved once. Who by? Can't remember.
Love dissolves like foam. I'm a skull with wings.
I run my thumb over the world –

does that hurt? It should.
I'm everything without a core.
Messy Robin, tide-of-garbage,
savage river, sunless sea.
Sweaty and shivery, hateful and sozzled,
Slept-in-the-Woods
and Things-Done-to-Me Robin.
A boy, fourteen, from Phrygia.
The world is full of big cats and reproach.
They're after me. Fox, where are you?

She's here, she's coming. Her yellow eyes,
her white-tipped brush and pointed mask
are the only thing Robin can recognise
as his. This is my night, the twenty-four hours
when silence has a voice. Can I get Robin
to give up a life apart? Christmas is a tightrope:
rejected is its heart – but so
is *light in the dark*. He's not alone.
Let him see light arrive across the globe.
A world more possible, and brighter, than he knows.

The night ahead will ebb and flow –
a night of vigil, stations of the soul,
an old truth dawning, a lightening of time
until, before the morning,
we might gaze at this bent world
with a blaze of hope
from absolutely nowhere. Come with me
into longed-for. Into all we can imagine
of mystery, wonder, hope, despair –
and a world, many worlds, elsewhere.

CHRISTMAS NIGHT

Holly Dreams Sunrise in East Australia

T *he sooner you sleep*, Mum said,
  the sooner tomorrow will come.
Holly's brother Sam
fell asleep at once but Holly's legs
want to bicycle and run. She tries
but she's camping in the air bed, on the floor,

and can't get comfortable. Her eyes
will not stay closed: Star
Hopper's gold mane glows
too bright from light under the door.
The empty stockings dangle in the dark
above the outline of Sam's *Airfix Cutty Sark*.

        Dad's locked the room
                the Christmas tree, presents and surprise
                        are out of bounds
        mustn't open the stockings
                or make a sound
                        till sunrise.

While she waits for sunrise in the black brocade
of London night, the first quiet songs
start up in the tropical dawn chorus
in the Queensland Everglades. A white haze
glows above a sea of smoky quartz
on the Sunshine Coast in East Australia

and a cone of ivory and pearl
comes into view on the silky black horizon.
Look Holly! A kangaroo, in a blaze
of primrose and dove-grey
light, is hopping through a swirl
of shallow, suddenly dazzling waves.

That's it. She's away
                and smiling
                        in her dream.

Robin Under Blackfriars Bridge

This shall be a sign? Robin's hiding from the rain
under a bridge. Those carols: was he ever
happy? *That's what I want. A sign.*
He's looking at the swill of the River Fleet

where it rushes out from underground
and splashes into Thames:
once a Roman waterway, then a tidal stream
and string of Anglo-Saxon wells

and now a sewage conduit, invisible
on the surface as the buried dreams
Robin clung to as a boy. But it still
flows on, under Fleet Street, Old Seacoal Lane

and four miles of the City.
That's a sign, but Robin
doesn't see it. If you touched him
with a straw he'd fall apart.

Christmas is slaughter.
Rubbish in the river
and everyone against me from the start.
Better to throw myself in dragon water.

His fox is sitting by, ears flat
against her skull. Robin –
You want a sign? I'll send you one!
The hankerings you once had

after sunlight and kind faces
are still yours, still you. Christmas is a wind
that blows people together.
Let the fox lead you to sanctuary and shelter.

He isn't sure he heard (am I in his head?)
but he's turned and, look, he's following the fox.
He trusts her. Let her talk to him
in whatever code they've made

in that mysterious link of human-animal.
Up White Lion Hill, sleet has turned to snow
and Robin's looking back at the blue-lit snake
of the bridge across the river – a neon glow

of mauve beneath and gold windows
behind like gridded teeth: a million
Peeping Toms in high-rise offices and flats
above the water's black, seductive Tao to oblivion…

No. The fox has pulled him on
up the hidden course of Fleet,
picking her way, paws slipping
on hardening ice, brush dipping

over the kerb of St Paul's Churchyard,
black on white, a pedestrian shadow-zone
of coffee-shops. Robin looks up
at the birthday-cake cathedral dome,

silver against the night. Firework-effect
festoons of lights from a municipal Christmas tree,
reflected in wet jewelled cracks of Purbeck stone,
stream to his feet like star-trails over sea.

She leads him to an arch, protected
from the wind. Robin shuts his eyes. All still
but blowing snow. As sunrise spreads
across the world, let Robin see the Christmas festival

through other lives, and know he's not alone:
that he belongs. He's the heart
of the Christmas under-song.
Outcast, and hope, and searching in the dark.

Sunrise Over Bethlehem

*A*s Robin sleeps in Aldersgate, the dawn creeps on
      and dazzle flows across the turning globe
through South-East Asia and India to Iran.
The snows of Damavand Volcano
redden into coral above the Caspian Sea,
on Nineveh Plain the solar azimuth is rose
and lavender, and now full sunlight glows
through clouds of dust from broken churches
in Qaraqosh, Christian capital of Iraq.
No Christmas under Isil. Sunrise here
lays bare the ancient citadel of Erbil
and ten thousand sagging tents for refugees –

where, look,
        someone has set up
                        in the snow
                                a Christmas tree

 and a crèche
        a candle-lit
                life-size Nativity
                        in a blue waterproof tepee.

Here in London, Robin wakes – the snow
is drifting now, he's frozen – and struggles to his feet.
He limps after the fox like a weary king
chasing a distant star, falls again
in a doorway, stares through whirling flakes
at the Central Criminal Court, Old Bailey,
and shuts his eyes just as the sun
is coming up in the Judaean mountains
two thousand feet above the sea
on Bethlehem. Let Robin dream
of the small, white, plateau town
where Christmas, whatever it means, began –

the place of birth, worshipping parents
and sweet smell of hay. A stable door ajar,
unexpected gifts, a sudden-standing star,
the budding out of love, the promise
of everything perfect on this earth.
Here's the actual place, under a winter sky
of broken lace, with a cloud like a giant bird
dancing on a skyline of silhouettes:
the Residence, the Omar Mosque
and Church of the Nativity, its gilt cross
touched by the hidden sun
spilling through purple cumulus.

This is my night to speak, I have to show
the truth. Nothing glossed over. Here too, look,
is the Separation Barrier. Robin knows
about *kept out* and *boxed in*.
The rising sun is sparkling on
a hostile settlement and eight-metre-high wall
of concrete, watchtowers, razor wire,
glinting metal, searchlights
and a shoot-at-sight militia
above and all around this little town.

And yet, just hours ago, thousands of pilgrims,
from all corners of the earth, pressed
into Manger Square and the holiest church
in Christendom, to celebrate
the sacrament of wine and bread,
the moment of God's birth.
The Patriarch called on Jews, Muslims
and Christians to live together equal
in this holy land. I heard his prayer:
may the New Year be better –
No barriers. Bridges of peace instead.

That's Bethlehem today. Spin the hour-glass,
what was *then*? I could say, the night
that blessed babe was born
it was raining cats and dogs. We alarmed
the shepherds tossing our shafts of light
through olive trees and pelting rain.
They turned up drenched, the barn roof leaked
and the whole place stank of cattle dung,
wet wool and rotting straw.
Or say, No, the sky was cloudless,
the air was soft and sweet. A moon,
like a milk-white bitten apple, on the wane.

Tell it how you like, it comes to the same
thing: a baby, displaced parents and their midnight
visitors from opposite walks of life.
Shepherds but also kings, the not-so-wise
wise men who brought rich gifts
and triggered a massacre.
All the children of Bethlehem
and the coasts thereof. The family became
refugees, seeking asylum.
Robin, listen closely in your sleep.
This touches you, doesn't it? Christmas
is children, gift-giving, persecution – and lost sheep.

The Christmas sun
is rising like rubbed gold
on hemmed-in Bethlehem

but Robin is free to move.
The snow has stopped.
He has the freedom of the night

to choose. To follow his star
his fox
into the light.

Dark, Pagan, Forbidden

*T*he clock in the hall strikes five. On the floor
    Holly half-wakes and then slips back
into her satchel of sleep as Robin's feet,
following paw-prints of the fox,
crunch through an inch of snow.
She's waiting for him at the shadowy maw
of Smithfield Market, normally in full swing
from 2 a.m.; tonight the black
empty ribcage of a dinosaur. Robin sinks
on a column plinth. There is a world elsewhere
but it's beyond his reach. Cut off and alone,
the way he's lived, feel more secure.

Above him, girders rise into the dark.
Drifting flakes seep into crevices, white
on white, and icy winds
hiss like a force of darkness. This is a night
of devilment. Sooty hobgoblins
of the hearth, the Wild Hunt, and all our old
forgotten demons rushing out to haunt us.
Not all Christmas gift-bringers are kind.
The Companions of Saint Nicholas,

Black Pete with his birch rod,
goat-horned Krampus, don't give sweets
but thrashings and lumps of coal.

Pagan Christmas fizzes and teems with ghosts,
midwinter fires, mummers and waites, Yule
logs and mistletoe. Everyone plays the fool
in a twelve-day free-for-all. Street plays,
dicing and dancing in every town,
pipers in masks and paper crowns
chasing the devil to put salt upon his tail,
whole swans roasting on spits, plum
pottage, brawn, and barrels of Christmas ale
while the Christmas King,
Lord of Misrule
turns all truth upside down.

Nothing to do with where Christmas began,
the windswept hills, wild thyme
and pale blue skies of Palestine.
This was Christmas for the northern hemisphere,
light in the dark at winter solstice
and everything topsy-turvy in the darkest time of year.

And then, in the Puritans' Republic, all this was forbidden.
Christmas was Catholic! *Easter* was the proper feast
for Protestants to celebrate. For fifteen years after a Civil War
it was illegal to sing carols, preach a Christmas sermon,
decorate a church with rosemary and bay.
Revellers, priests and worshippers were tortured, jailed
and put to death. Yet everyone kept Christmas Day
in secret: banning Christmas failed. People made
the moment festive and holy as they'd known it.
When shops on Cheapside opened, gangs of young
apprentices with cudgels rioted and forced them shut.
Still, those were England's missing years of Christmas fun.

> Robin is opening his eyes. Does this remind
> him of himself? The fox is trying to push him up
> and on. Does he realise what he left behind,
> retreating to his would-be deaf and dumb
> where he could not be touched?
> Something has chimed...

Robin Remembers Firelight

Missing years? The snow cracks soft,
like biscuit. I remember slippy pavements.
I was small, I was hardly there, I was hardly me,
walking with my dad to buy a tree.
Dad, yes, teaching me to make a fire,
a red glow at the heart
and blossom yellow flames. We laughed.

Did we laugh, really? No. I came to life
through a winter door. Dad died –
Mum said, though I was never sure
what she said was true. Step-dad
was clouts on the head and crying in the dark.
Ran off, didn't I? Got free. But they're still there,
still at me with their cudgels. Still after me.

Sunrise Over Rome

R obin slithers on. This is the darkest moment
before dawn. While the sun
is gliding west, closer to home,

I want to show him one last thing:
the boy he saw from Phrygia
with a leopard at his feet. Pancras,

who lived in Rome. Come through the arch
in this red wall on the Janiculum
along an avenue of bare, gnarled trees

to San Pancrazio's Basilica
where every morning priests feed refugees
from Libya and Syria

and now they're moving chairs
to set a Christmas table.
Everything round here,

apartment blocks, the roads and infrastructure
is in disrepair, but charity,
taking care of those in need,

has been part of Christmas from the start
and San Pancrazio, patron saint
of children, is at the heart of Christianity.

Pancras was fourteen. Like you, Robin,
when you ran away. An orphan
brought to Rome from Turkey

seventeen centuries ago. He refused
to sacrifice to the Romans' gods
so they sent him to the Coliseum,

to the Games, where that leopard
would not savage him until the boy
gave permission. He was buried in a catacomb

whose stacked-up tombs held bones
of Eastern Christians who had fled to Rome
escaping massacre and persecution.

Pancrazio was their own brave
Eastern boy. Over his tomb
they built this red basilica.

You too, Robin, should trust your own
idea of good: whatever's in you
that can seek, and find, a home.

Dark mottled cloud hangs in the sky like moss
above a jigsaw of spires and domes
but in the east, a wavy smudge
of fluorescent orange runs
like livid paint across
the rising line of black pine trees
and candelabra of St Peter's.

One final sign: a vision of the sun,
still under the horizon, pushing
a gilded semi-circle
over the holy city
which the real thing
will move up into as it comes.
A halo of gold leaf for the Nativity.

Robin Finds His Voice

Imagine sun... Robin is half-blind
with ice-crust on his lashes. The world
is going on. In the dark he nearly falls

up snow-cushioned steps to a set-back hall
and blue door with a sign.
CARING AT CHRISTMAS. The fox stays in the snow.

Pricked ears. All quickness stilled
to that topaz yellow, waiting-to-see-
what-you'll-do-next fox stare.

Will Robin dare? *Never before...*
Danger... Forbidden...
Robin! Push the door!

     A strip-lit corridor, a shiny floor
     and a woman stirring soup.

     Let's dry your hair
     and get this round you. Here.

Buzzing lights. Fluorescent glare.
Then a blanket over him, a mantle.
He's sitting on a chair. His feet begin to steam.

He's seeing, forty years ago, white pillows
in corners of a window-frame –
a forgotten dream of fire-lit snow, and a kitchen

where his mother, yes, his mum, not drunk, just gentle,
everything in bud, is making a real cake. Love,
and the lack of it, can change the limbic brain.

> The Crisis Centre woman brings a tray
> with tea, sugar, bread and soup.

> Robin hasn't spoken words out loud
> for years. What can cracked, blue,

> cold-sore-scarred lips do?
> He opens them. *Who are you?*

CHRISTMAS DAY

Luminous

This looks like London night still, but it isn't.
Chains of street lights vanish one by one.
A distant clock strikes seven. The cold
could numb your face, your breath
coils out in the freezing air like smoke
and from where I am the River Thames
looks like a platinum ribbon. The frosted spikes
of Gherkin, Cheesegrater and Shard
rise into paling cloud. The Eye is motionless:
a filigree wheel, jutting into sky as if to cage
the brightening arc of corona rays,
magenta, rosé, lemon, before we see the sun.

Holly wakes in the air-bed on the floor
and gazes through familiar shadows
at two filled stockings by the door.
Bulging, mysterious… But she mustn't touch,
not yet. Their house hasn't got a chimney
so how did Father Christmas – ? Who is he, anyway?
What's real, at Christmas? Has the sun come up?
She slithers from the duvet, lifts the blind
and gasps at a magic world. Still dark

but everything is white, as if a luminous
wind of foam has passed over the grass,
over everything, in the night.

Behind the shed, the laden hedge
is softly lumpy. Nothing green
and nothing sharp. Even in the dark, each twig
has its own coating of ice-cream.
This is what whispering would look like
if you drew it. Milk fur. Untouched.
And all, this moment, just for her.
But something red, a flame, an animal,
maybe a ginger cat, is slinking out of sight
behind the shed. Then Holly sees a line
of primrose light. Sunrise! Quick, wake
Sam, make a snowman, find the sledge!

But first, the stockings. Sam lifts them down.
They open them in his bed. Daylight falls
on a muddle of cellophane and Crazy Foam,
Glow-in-Dark Skeletons, Cola Balls,
Pokemon cards, a Wind-Powered

Paper Glider and a My Little Pony comb.
They hunt for outdoor clothes through a crackly storm
of wrapping-paper. The garden is soft and hushed:
magic, as Holly saw it by herself,
but different with someone else. Snow showers,
snowballs, a snowman. And a secret line
of animal tracks like small black flowers.

Fake Logs, Real Flames

From where you are
                you hear

the flutters
        of Holly's longing.

What do you make
                when you make believe?

Tissue paper
        Christmas tree

fake logs
        real flames

a yellow and blue
                plastic stable for her ponies

ballet shoes
        and video games

but no
    no wish-come-true

life-long friend.
      No puppy.

The Wild Oat

*I*n the Crisis Centre, behind a tinsel tree,
frying-pans are spitting and kettles roar
in a kitchenette. Outside, one star
tangled in leafless branches of a sycamore
fades into afternoon while Robin sleeps

and wakes to the fragile clockwork of his heart.
He's a lightning-blasted tree, a wild oat.
As a child, he lived with demons.
Now he sees a red formica table. A spread
of roast potatoes, turkey, gravy, bread.

A woman in pink washes Robin's hair,
manicures his bitten nails,
gives him a fizzy drink. A henna angel.
For the first time in years
he's touched by someone else.

My name is Mesoma, darling.
Mesoma means God's Blessing.
I'm from Nigeria.
You have lovely hair. It's strong
and soft. You ready to eat, again?

If the soul asks, *Is it far?*
you say, on the far side of the mirror.
Across the hidden river. Not this side but that.

For the first time Robin is seeing through
the outer layers of someone else
to light beneath. A sad light – she's hurt too:

Mesoma-Means-God's-Blessing volunteered
at a Christmas Crisis Centre
because her boyfriend left her.

Half-cough, half-croak, Robin unlocks
the calyx of his throat.
Gotta take food to Fox.

Scraps in a plastic bag. Echoes of their feet
in frozen streets. All over town,
children are throwing snowballs,

trying out the X-box
or the trampoline, as parents watch
the Queen's Speech on TV.

If the soul asks, *Is it far?*
you say, on the far side of the mirror.
Across the hidden river. Not that side but this.

*C*ome with me into dying light. The day
is nearly over, the sun low on the horizon
and my twenty-four hours of speech
are near the end. Almost the moment to release
silence back into silence. Robin has returned
to St Pancras Old Church, the River Fleet
flows on beneath and the woman
who has walked into Robin's story
is helping him search for Fox. The snow
is melting slush. Across the way, nurses
in Accident & Emergency are changing shift
inside the rose-red brick of St Pancras Hospital.

Mesoma-Means-God's-Blessing touches Robin's arm
and points across the road to the long-stay
hostel, where Robin could sleep warm,
maybe rebuild his life. *You should go in.*
    He has lived his days in narrowing light,
    with someone gift-bringers.
    someone ed on his side.
            has changed.

                        ing.

He'll find the fox, give her food
and come back with his things.

I'll wait in the church, she says. *I'll pray*
for me, also for you. At the moon-rim
of her smile, a peal of bells
starts ringing in the tower. Christmas
is seeing, suddenly, what's hidden,
looking for the unknown thing
which will make your life worthwhile
and not looking away from suffering.
Robin walks on, nothing feels forbidden
now, across the buried river
and on past Goldington Crescent Park
where Holly, last night, saw him sitting in the dark.

The Gift of Fox

*H*olly comes out into the garden
　　and the dulling diamond of afternoon
alone. To play in the snow, she says. Really to cry
at not having a puppy. Christmas is a wild ride
for everyone. The light is grainy dusk,
the snow is trodden, blackened, nearly gone –

like everything she ever wanted. Grim
twilight, murk, and slush…
Suddenly by the hedge, behind the shed,
she sees a stranger with grey floaty locks
like cartoon Merlin from the *Once and Future King*.
He's bending down to feed a fox. Holly stares.

The dream-stranger moves jerkily as if on strings.
The fox doesn't care – it eats a chicken wing
from his fingers, throws the bone up in the air
and pounces on it like a kitten. The stranger laughs.
Holly doesn't breathe. What she thought immovable,
a pile of withered bramble, has been rolled away.

Under the shed her dad built is a hole, a cavern.
She takes a step. As her light-up shoes sparkle
the stranger and the fox see her and go still.

Well now. Listen. In the fading light
Holly sees a magician. Robin is trying to say
goodbye to Fox. He has no idea I've been with him
all night but here's another vision, a figure with
   a tangle
of gold curls and starlit feet. It might sprout wings
any moment. Robin sees an angel.

Who are you?
        I'm leaving now.
Is that fox yours?
        She's my friend.

Robin takes the muzzle between his hands,
teases the pointed ears.
Her eyes in his. A farewell barely spoken.
Loneliness, the path of longing,
not getting what you hoped for
but maybe something else, is taking flight.

Flow on, flow on. I'm holding my breath too.
As the buried river moves beneath our feet
Robin is giving up all he's known.
He hefts his rucksack, hesitates.
Then Holly's magician passes into
shadowlands, leaving Holly and fox alone.

I'm not his fox. I'm my own fox.
But I could be your friend.
In a second, Holly somersaults

to a world she always knew
was waiting. The place
where foxes talk.

You'll bring me food?
  Yes. Every day.
You won't see me all the time.

You'll seek me and not find.
But I'm around, I'm here.
  Okay.

Look, Holly's reaching out her hand. Very gingerly –
who's shyer? – a tongue touches her skin.
This is better than her dream. Not a puppy

but a fox. A talking fox. The dying light
is blue as a welder's flame
then violet, amber, silver. Tangerine.

Sunrise on Liberty Island

*L*ast embers of the sunset turn the stone
    of St Pancras Old Church to dusky hellebore.
In this realm, for now, I'm done.
Twilight is here, the day must close
and my voice stop for another year.
Robin puts his hand to the hostel door
as other doors far away are opening
and the gold wing of Christmas dawn
sweeps the Atlantic, glowing on terracotta
roof-tops of Natal, north-east Brazil,
and flushing the topmost spires
of the tallest buildings in Manhattan –

where someone, down in the fading dark
and brightening-to-citron morning light,
is singing *O Little Town of Bethlehem.*
The sun climbs over Liberty State Park,
New York Harbour and the waterfront

until a torque of fretted gold
blazes from the sea
behind the colossus silhouette
of *Liberty Enlightening the World*
and sparkles on her torch-welcome to immigrants

and her crown of seven sunrays, chosen
for seven continents and seven seas
because her maker dreamed that freedom
would now be universal. The Christmas sun
throws tiny shadows into a kaleidoscope
of letters cast in bronze upon her pedestal.
Send me your homeless. Yearning to breathe free.
Let that hope shine on, like the wheel
of a rare fire rainbow in a circumhorizontal arc
above the sleeping harbour, while I fall
silent and you step back into the dark
transforming world where time, once more, is real.

Acknowledgements

Many warm thanks to members of *Kindlings*, Phillip Birch, Jane Davies, Mike Dibb, Cheli Duran and Aamer Hussein, for invaluable comments on inchoate drafts. Also to my colleague Declan Ryan for great close comments and for always being available to help think, and to Gwen Burnyeat and Bill Carslake for insights and reactions at home (and sometimes from abroad), for listening, comments and endlessly generative discussions, especially of journeys and angels.

Many thanks to 'Signor Catacomb' at San Pancrazio in Rome, who showed me round the catacombs. Also to Cill Rialaig artists' retreat on Bolus Head, Co Kerry where I wrote the second draft and to Daphne Astor, who was writing there too and offered invaluable comments on each new instalment every night.

Many thanks also to Sushrut Jadhav who by saying 'What about places where Christmas is forbidden?' set off the outcast, forbidden and persecuted theme, and who took the time, one bitterly cold night just after Christmas, to walk me round and into homeless hostels throughout Camden and introduce me to wonderful people at many different Receptions. I apologize to him that for purposes of shaping I had to cut a passage on Christmas in India set in Mahad, Maharashtra, where on Christmas Day 1927 Ambedkar burned the 2000-year-old law book, the *Manusmriti*, enshrining the caste system.

Finally, I can't thank my editor Parisa Ebrahimi enough for her inspiration, encouragement, her close critical insights at macro and micro level, and her extraordinary patience.